D1440396

Hall of Fame

Old Testament

HALL OF FAME OLD TESTAMENT

 Enoch
(Genesis 5:18-32;
Hebrews 11:5-6)

 Jochabed
(Exodus 1 and 2)

 Jethro
(Exodus 18)

 Bezalel & Oholiab
(Exodus 35 - 38)

 Caleb
(Numbers 13:30)

 Rahab
(Joshua 2; Hebrews 11:31)

 Naomi
(Ruth 1-4)

 Abigail
(1 Samuel 25)

 Mephibosheth
(2 Samuel 9)

 Barzillai
(2 Samuel 19:31-39)

 Asa
(1 Kings 15;
2 Chronicles 14)

 Obadiah
(1 Kings 18)

Naboth
(1 Kings 21)

 Micaiah
(1 Kings 22;
2 Chronicles 18)

 The Shunammite woman
(2 Kings 4)

 Captive Maid
(2 Kings 5:1-4)

 Joash
(2 Kings 11;
2 Chronicles 22)

 Hezekiah
(2 Kings 18-19;2
Chronicles 31:20-21;)

 Jabez
(1 Chronicles 4:9-10)

 Jehoshaphat
(2 Chronicles 19)

 Mordecai
(Esther 2 and 6)

 Ebed Melech
(Jeremiah 38)

Enoch (Genesis 5:18-32; Hebrews 11:5-6)

Enoch is a character that you will find quite near the beginning of the Bible. However, he is only mentioned two or three times in the whole of the Bible. Enoch's story is mentioned in the book of Genesis and in the book of Hebrews. So why is he here in this *Hall of Fame*? From the little that is mentioned about Enoch in the Bible here is what we have discovered about him.

Enoch is actually an ancestor of another famous Bible character, Noah. Noah was a key player in God's dramatic rescue mission from the flood that covered the whole earth. Enoch was Noah's great grandfather.

Enoch is also well known because he was the father of Methuselah. Methuselah lived a very long time. He was 969 years old when he died. But Enoch is not in the Hall of Fame because of any of his relatives or because his son lived to a record breaking age. The most interesting thing that happened to Enoch is that he walked with God.

Enoch was well known for being a man who pleased God. Enoch spent lots of time speaking with God and listening to him. Enoch loved to be with God. They were very close and were very good friends. Enoch has also gained a place in this *Hall of Fame* because of the way he died. When Enoch was 365 years old God decided that it was time for Enoch to go to heaven to be with him all the time. Did Enoch fall sick? Did he injure himself? No. Then how did he die?

God took Enoch's soul and body straight to heaven. Normally when you die your body stays behind, but with Enoch it was different. Enoch had a special friendship with God so God took him home to heaven in a special way. Enoch pleased God. He had faith in God. The Bible tells us that without faith it is impossible to please God.

TopTip: *Spend time with God just like Enoch did.*
'Blessed are all who respect God and walk in his ways.' Psalm 128:1

Jochabed (Exodus 1 and 2)

Jochabed was a brave and clever mum. Her husband was called Amram. She had a daughter called Miriam and a son called Aaron. Then she gave birth to another bouncing, baby boy. But Jochabed's people were Egyptian slaves. Pharaoh, the ruler of Egypt, ordered that all Hebrew baby boys should be thrown into the River Nile. Jochabed hid her baby until he got too big and noisy to hide in the house.

Then she hid him in a special waterproof basket and placed the basket amongst the reeds by the river. The baby's sister, Miriam, stayed to watch over him and was there when Pharaoh's daughter came to the river to bathe. Pharaoh's daughter found the baby and felt sorry for him.

Miriam, who was clever like her mum, ran out to ask the princess if she would like someone to help her look after the baby. The princess thought it was a great idea and Miriam ran to fetch... you've guessed it... Jochabed.

So not only did Jochabed's plan to save her baby succeed, Miriam's plan to get her baby brother back was a success as well.

The Egyptian princess even paid Jochabed to look after the baby for her. But God was the real brains behind the whole operation. His plans always come together. The princess named the baby Moses. Perhaps you have heard of him? When he got to a certain age he left to live in the Egyptian Palace. He grew up to be a great hero himself and a mighty man of God.

Top Tip: *Trust in God and in his plans for your life.* 'Trust in the Lord with all your heart. Lean not on your own understanding. In all your ways acknowledge him and he will make your paths straight.' Proverbs 3:5-6

Jethro (Exodus 18)

Jethro was a wise man who respected God. He was also Moses' father in law. After Moses had been used by God to free the Hebrew people from slavery, God put Moses in charge. Moses had to sort out all the squabbles and difficulties that the people had with one another. One day Moses thought it would be good to see Jethro again. He longed to tell him the amazing story about how God had helped the Hebrew people escape from the Egyptians.

Moses sent his wife Zipporah and their two sons, Gershom and Eliezer, to see Jethro who lived in Midian. When they returned they brought Jethro with them. Jethro was delighted to hear about the amazing things that God had done. 'Now I know that the the Lord is greater than all other Gods!' he exclaimed.

But Jethro was surprised at the amount of work poor Moses had to do. From morning until night Moses was busy sorting out everybody's problems. 'You are going to wear yourself out, Moses,' he warned. Jethro gave Moses some good advice. 'Teach the people God's laws and show them how to live. Select capable and honest men who respect God. Make each responsible for a certain number of people.'

Jethro continued, 'Some can be in charge of ten people others a hundred and still others can be in charge of 1000 people or more. They can then sort out the day to day problems. The more difficult problems will be brought to you. If God thinks this is a good idea you should do this. It will make your job easier and the people will get their problems sorted out much quicker. Everybody will be satisfied.'

Moses did this. He agreed that it was a very sensible idea.

Top Tip: *Always ask God to show you what to do.*
'God's word is a lamp to my feet and a light to my path.' Psalm 119:105

Bezalel and Oholiab (Exodus 35 - 38)

Bezalel and Oholiab were very talented. They were so talented that they were both chosen to do very important jobs. God chose them to oversee the design of the Tabernacle - the special place where God's people came to worship him. It was important to get just the right people to work on the Tabernacle and only the very best materials were used.

God instructed Moses about how the Tabernacle should look and God knew exactly who the best people were to oversee the project. God wanted Bezalel and Oholiab because he had given them special gifts. It was only right that they used the gifts God gave them to make God's special place a wonderful and beautiful place to be.

What were Bezalel and Oholiab good at? They were top class artists and craftsmen. Bezalel made amazing things with gold, silver and bronze. Both Bezalel and Oholiab were experts at embroidery and weaving.

Bezalel and Oholiab had to teach others how to do the intricate crafts and embroidery too. This was important because they couldn't do the whole job themselves. Bezalel and Oholiab made beautiful curtains out of blue, scarlet and purple yarn. Golden ornaments and other items such as lamps, tables, dishes and bowls were also made.

Bezalel was given a particularly special job - he was responsible for making the Ark of the Covenant. This was a chest made from Acacia wood and covered with pure gold inside and out. God's Law was placed inside the chest - it was a very important part of the whole Tabernacle.

Top Tip: *Work hard and try your very best!*
'Whatever your hand finds to do - do it with all your might. '
Ecclesiastes 9:10

Caleb (Numbers 13:30)

Have you ever imagined what it is like to be a spy? The Israelite spies spied on the land of Canaan. God had promised to give it to them as a home of their own. When the spies returned from their explorations some gave the following report: 'The land is fertile. Look at the fruit we have brought back. But the people there are very strong. Their cities are walled and very large. We even saw giants there.'

One spy, Caleb, heard the reports and wasn't pleased. They gave a wrong impression.

Caleb spoke up, 'Be quiet! We should go and take possession of this land. We can certainly do it!' But nothing would change their minds. 'We can't attack them. They are stronger than us. They are so big that we felt like grasshoppers beside them,' the other people argued.

Caleb urged them not to give up. 'The land is very good. If the Lord is pleased with us he will give it to us. Do not turn against him. Don't be afraid of the people in that land. We will defeat them utterly. They have no protection but the Lord is with us.' But the people would not change their minds so God was angry with them.

God told the Israelites that they would never live to see Canaan. They would spend the rest of their lives in the desert. When they had died their children would be allowed to enter the land of Canaan and defeat it.

But Caleb had thought differently from the other people. He had followed God completely. God promised that Caleb would see the land of Canaan once again. He promised to reward him and his family with land and property when they finally arrived there.

Top Tip: *Stand up for the truth.*
'I have chosen the way of truth.' Psalm 119:30

Rahab (Joshua 2; Hebrews 11:31)

Rahab lived in Canaan in the city of Jericho. But Jericho was being spied on. The Israelites were being helped by God to defeat their enemies and take over the land. Rahab decided it was better to be on the side of God, rather than supporting sin and God's enemies, so she helped the Israelites. She even helped two Israelite spies to escape capture from the Jericho soldiers.

She sent the soldiers on a wild goose chase by telling them that the spies had been at her house but they had just left. 'Hurry. You might catch up with them!' she exclaimed. The soldiers didn't know that the two spies were hiding on Rahab's roof all the time. She had covered them with a pile of flax to keep them hidden.

The spies promised Rahab that they would protect her and her family when the Israelites attacked the city. All she had to do was hang a scarlet cord out the window of her house so that the Israelites would know not to attack that building.

Rahab's house was built into the side of the city walls so she lowered the spies through a window down to the ground on the other side.

When the Israelites defeated Jericho, Rahab and her family were safe. She was then allowed to live with the Israelites and even married an Israelite man. Eventually she became the great-great grandmother of King David.

 Top Tip: *Always obey God even though it might make your life difficult. God honours those who obey him and who give their lifes to him.*
'Those who honour me I will honour' 1 Samuel 2:30

Naomi (Ruth 1 - 4)

Naomi's story is a sad one but it has a happy ending. Naomi was a Jewish wife and mother who lived in the town of Bethlehem with her husband, Elimelech, and her two sons, Mahlon and Kilion. But her family left Bethlehem because of a bad famine. They travelled to the land of Moab where food was more plentiful. After they settled there Elimelech died and Naomi's two sons married two native women - Orpah and Ruth. Ten years later tragedy struck again. Naomi's sons died leaving the three women to look after themselves.

Naomi then heard that God had stopped the famine in Bethlehem. She decided to return there. Naomi told Ruth and Orpah to go home to their families but Ruth and Orpah both began to cry. They didn't want to leave Naomi. Orpah eventually agreed to return but Ruth refused. She said, 'Don't ask me to leave you. Where you go, I will go. Where you live, I will live. Your people will be my people and your God my God. Where you die, I will die and there I will be buried. God will punish me if I do not keep this promise. Not even death will separate us.'

In Bethlehem Ruth was a great help to Naomi. She went to the fields to gather loose corn that was of no use to the farmers. Ruth then met Boaz, Naomi's relative, and Naomi knew Boaz would make Ruth a good husband. She hatched a plan to bring them both together. Eventually Boaz and Ruth married and when Ruth gave birth to a son called Obed, Naomi had a proper family again. Naomi loved Obed and would give him lots of cuddles. Obed also had a grandson many years later called David. He became a great king in Israel.

 Top Tip: *Thank God for the good things he has given you. Trust him to work things out.*
'The Lord gives many blessings to all who trust in him.' Romans 10:12

Abigail (1 Samuel 25)

Abigail was intelligent and beautiful. Her husband Nabal was surly and mean. Abigail's story begins when David and his men needed some supplies. Nabal owed David a favour. Once David and his men had been kind to Nabal's shepherds by helping to look after their sheep. David was sure Nabal would give them supplies as it was sheep shearing time and everyone would be in a festive mood. However, Nabal was not in a festive mood. He accused David and his men of being runaway slaves. When the men returned empty handed David told his men to get ready to fight.

Abigail realised Nabal had been foolish. David was a warrior. A lot of people would die if she didn't do something. Hurriedly she gathered 200 loaves of bread, 2 large containers of wine, 5 sheep ready for roasting, 5 measures of roasted grain, 100 raisin cakes and 200 fig cakes. She loaded these onto donkeys and Abigail and her servants hurried to meet David. David was just about to attack when Abigail arrived. She apologised for Nabal's behaviour and pleaded with David not to attack them. 'When God makes you leader over Israel you will not feel guilty because you killed innocent people.'

David told Abigail to go in peace to her house. 'May you be blessed for your wisdom. You have kept me from killing people today. I have listened to what you have said and respect you for it.' When Nabal heard what had happened he got such a shock that he collapsed on the spot and ten days later he died. So Abigail was used by God to stop David from killing innocent people and she eventually became David's wife.

 Top Tip: *Be wise!* 'If you need wisdom ask God for it. He is generous and ... he will give you wisdom.' James 1: 5
'Wisdom begins with respect for God and understanding begins with knowing the Holy one.' Proverbs 9:10

Mephibosheth (2 Samuel 9)

Mephibosheth is quite a mouthful to say but something amazing happened to him. When David was a young warrior, King Saul was very jealous of David's success and he gradually came to hate David. Saul was disobedient to God and God was very displeased with him.

Saul's son, Jonathan, was David's best friend. He helped David escape from his father Saul who wanted to kill him. David promised that as long as Jonathan lived he would show God's kindness to him. He also promised to show kindness to Jonathan's family.

One day Saul and Jonathan were killed in a battle against the Philistines. David now ruled over Israel, as he was chosen by God. David remembered his promise to Jonathan and decided to find out if any of Jonathan's family had survived. He found a servant, called Ziba, who had been employed by Saul's family. David asked Ziba about Jonathan's family. Ziba replied that Jonathan's son was alive but was crippled in both his feet, 'His name is Mephibosheth and he lives at the house of Makir in Lo Debar.'

When Mephibosheth saw David he bowed down before the king but David said, 'Don't be afraid. I will be kind to you because of Jonathan your father. I will give you back all the land of your grandfather Saul, and you will always eat at my table.'

Ziba, the servant, was put in charge of farming Mephibosheth's land so Mephibosheth could stay in Jerusalem and ate at the king's table just like a member of the Royal family. He was well looked after. David had kept his promise to his best friend, Jonathan.

Top Tip: *We should show other people how kind God is by being kind ourselves. Remember how kind God was to us by reading John 3:16.* 'I will tell of the kindness of the Lord' Isaiah 63: 7.

Barzillai (2 Samuel 19:31-39)

Barzillai was a very old man. He was eighty years old. But he was well respected by King David. Why? Was he wealthy? Yes, he was, but this wasn't the reason David respected him. Was Barzillai a generous man? Did he share his wealth with King David? Yes, he did. Barzillai provided food and clothing and whatever David needed when David was staying with Barzillai at Mahanaim. But on top of all this Barzillai showed David that he was a trustworthy man. David could rely on Barzillai.

Once David was cruelly treated by his son Absalom. Absalom tried to get rid of his father David so that he could become king instead. The result was that there was a great battle between David and his supporters and Absalom and his supporters. Barzillai always supported David and never betrayed him. David knew that he could trust Barzillai. It was a great shame that David could not trust his own son. He was sad when Absalom was killed, but in the end he returned to Jerusalem and Barzillai was there to cheer him on his way.

Before he left, David asked Barzillai to come and live with him in Jerusalem but Barzillai wanted to stay at home. He didn't want to be a burden to King David. Barzillai didn't want to die in a strange place. Instead he asked David to take a man called Kimham instead. 'Anything you desire from me I will do for you,' David said to Barzillai. Then he turned to give his old friend Barzillai a kiss and a blessing. Barzillai must have been a very good friend indeed.

Top Tip: *Be loyal to your friends and to God. Make God the most important person in your life.*
'The Lord rewards people who are faithful and righteous.' 1 Samuel 26:23.

Asa (1 Kings 15; 2 Chronicles 14)

Asa is a descendant of King David. After David died his son, Solomon, became king and after Solomon died the kingdom split into two parts. The southern kingdom of Israel and the northern kingdom of Judah. Asa eventually became ruler of Judah and did some rather surprising things.

Asa's army was 580,000 brave fighting men with spears and shields, but one day Zerah from Cush came out to fight them and he had an enormous army and 300 chariots. Asa knew that they didn't stand a chance. So what did he do? Perhaps you think he should have retreated. However, Asa knew that his God was more powerful than the most powerful army, so he prayed to God.

'Lord, only you can help the weak against the strong. Help us, we depend on you. We fight against this enormous army in your name. You are our God. Don't let them defeat you.'

God answered Asa's prayer. He defeated the Cushites and their enormous army ran away. The Cushite army was defeated so soundly and so completely that it could never fight again.

God told the people of Judah that he would always be with them if they always fully trusted him. God also told Asa and his people to be strong and not to give up. Asa commanded the people to worship the one true God and all idols were removed and destroyed. He even destroyed the idols of his grandmother Macaah and because the people of Judah obeyed God they experienced a time of peace while Asa was king.

 Top Tip: *Always trust God. He is the only one you can always rely on.*
'It is better to trust in the Lord than to trust people. It is better to trust in the Lord than to trust in princes.' Psalm 118: 8-9

Obadiah (1 Kings 18)

Obadiah was a secret believer and was overseer of King Ahab and Queen Jezebel's palace. This was an important position but King Ahab and Queen Jezebel were not followers of the Lord God. They hated God and his people and worshipped a false god, called Baal instead. But Obadiah was not like them. He followed God and believed in him but King Ahab and Queen Jezebel did not know this. Because of this secrecy Obadiah was used by God to do an amazing thing. Obadiah rescued 100 of God's prophets.

When Jezebel was on a killing spree, killing as many of God's people as she could find, Obadiah took 100 prophets and hid them in caves. He put 50 prophets in one cave and 50 in another. He also kept them supplied with food and water. Isn't it amazing to think that Jezebel was busy looking around for prophets to kill, while right under her nose her chief servant was busy looking around for prophets to rescue? Obadiah was a true believer. He followed God and he showed this by his actions.

Obadiah knew the Prophet Elijah who also believed in God. The difference between them is that Elijah was known by Ahab and Jezebel as God's prophet. It is good to stand up for our belief in God and his son Jesus Christ. However, on certain occasions believers have to remain silent and worship God in secret. If we pray to God he will help us to know when to speak and when to be silent. God helps people who are like Elijah and people who are like Obadiah.

 Top Tip: *Do not be afraid of people. If you love Jesus, the bible tells us to...* 'Always be ready to answer everyone who asks you to explain about the hope you have.' 1 Peter 3:15.

Naboth (1 Kings 21)

Naboth's story is worth telling because it shows us how greed and sin can destroy life. Naboth owned a vineyard in Jezreel where King Ahab lived. Ahab had lots of vineyards but one day he saw Naboth's vineyard and thought, 'I would like to make that land into a vegetable garden. It is so near the palace. I'll ask Naboth to give it to me. I'll give him a better vineyard in its place or I will pay him for it.'

But Naboth didn't want to give the vineyard to the king. 'This vineyard belongs to my family. I am not going to sell it to you,' he said.

Ahab went home angry and upset. He went to bed and sulked. He refused to eat and lay with his face turned to the wall. Jezebel, Ahab's wife, came in to see what was the matter. 'Why are you refusing to eat?' she asked. Ahab whinged, 'I asked Naboth from Jezreel to sell me his vineyard. I offered him a better one in return, but Naboth refused!' Jezebel couldn't believe it, 'Is this how you rule your kingdom? Get up, eat something and be happy. I will get Naboth's vineyard for you.'

Jezebel hatched an evil plan. She wrote some important men in Naboth's town and told them to call the people together for a special day of prayer. Naboth was to be put between two trouble makers who would falsely accuse him of saying horrible things about God and King Ahab. Naboth would then be stoned to death.

Everything happened just as Jezebel instructed. But God saw it all! God told Elijah to go to Naboth's vineyard and tell Ahab that the Lord God knew what had happened and that Ahab and Jezebel would be punished.

 Top Tip: *Be content. Do not wish you had other people's possessions - be satisfied with what God has given you.*
Remember the commandment, 'Do not covet.' Deuteronomy 5:21.

Micaiah (1 Kings 22; 2 Chronicles 18)

What Micaiah did in this story was very brave indeed. He followed God when most people didn't listen to God at all.

Micaiah lived in the southern kingdom of Israel, when Ahab ruled Israel and Jehosaphat ruled Judah. Ahab and Jehosaphat came together to plan an attack on Ramoth in Gilead. But Jehosaphat first wanted them to check if this was what God wanted them to do. So Ahab called for 400 prophets and asked, 'Should we go to war against Ramoth in Gilead or not?'

Ahab was not a follower of the true God and neither were the prophets that he called. All the prophets said only what Ahab wanted to hear. 'You should fight the battle because God will let you win.' Jehosaphat wasn't entirely happy with this answer and asked whether there was still a prophet of the Lord left in Israel. 'Let's ask him what we should do.' King Ahab replied, 'There is one, but I hate him. He never says anything good about me. His name is Micaiah!' Ahab sent a messenger to Micaiah who urged him to say the same thing that all the other prophets had said.

But Micaiah would only say what God told him to say. So he told King Ahab that it was God's plan that he should go into the battle not because Ahab would win but because Ahab would be killed. Ahab flung Micaiah into prison but went into the battle in disguise just incase. As the battle went on an enemy soldier took an arrow and shot it haphazardly into the air. It landed just in between the pieces of Ahab's armour. He was fatally wounded and Micaiah had been right. Ahab died at sunset. We don't know what happened to Micaiah next. All we do know is that he told the truth and followed God.

 Top Tip: *Tell the truth even though it makes things difficult.*
'The truth will set you free.' John 8:32. 'Tell each other the truth' Zechariah 8:16.

Shunammite Woman (2 Kings 4)

We don't know this person's real name but we know that she lived in Shunem so that is why she is called the Shunammite woman. She looked after the prophet Elisha when he came through her town and she even built a special room for him on the top of her house. This room was nicely kitted out with a bed, table and chair as well as a little lamp to use when it got dark. Elisha was so thankful for all the nice things this woman had done for him that he wanted to do something for her in return. But she said that she had everything she needed.

However, Gehazi, Elisha's servant, had an idea. He told Elisha that even though the Shunammite woman was married she had never had any sons. Having sons was important in Israel at that time, as it meant that when the parents were old they would have someone to look after them and also carry on the work of the farm. Having a son meant that God had blessed your family. Elisha then called the Shunammite woman and said to her, 'This time next year you will have a son.' She didn't believe him but sure enough next year she had a baby boy.

One day the little boy's head began to hurt. He became very sick and died. His mother ran to find Elisha, who, when he arrived, went straight to the boy's room. He stretched himself across the dead body which began to grow warm. Then he stretched himself out across the boy one more time. The boy sneezed - seven times and opened his eyes. The Shunammite woman was overjoyed that her little boy was alive.

 Top Tip: *Believe in the power of God. Jesus Christ has the power to forgive your sins and to give you eternal life.*
'Great is our Lord and mighty in power.' Psalm 147:5

The Captive Maid (2 Kings 5:1-4)

We do not know this girl's name but we know that one day a troup of Aramean Soldiers raided her country of Israel and took her away captive. That is why we call her the captive maid. In the country of Aram at that time there was a great warrior and commander called Naaman. The King of Aram was pleased with Naaman because he had conquered many people. However, Naaman had a horrible skin disease, called leprosy, which was very unpleasant. When the captured girl arrived in Aram she ended up as a servant in Naaman's household, where she looked after his wife.

One day the maid remembered something from her homeland which she told her mistress about, 'I wish my master would go and see the prophet who lives in Samaria. He would cure him of his disease.' So Naaman asked the King of Aram for permission to go. The King gave Naaman a letter of introduction to the King of Israel which read, 'I am sending my servant Naaman to you so that you can cure him of his skin disease.' When the King of Israel read this he was really upset as he thought the King of Aram was telling him to cure Naaman, and he knew he couldn't do it. The prophet Elisha heard about the King's problem and came to the rescue. Elisha would see to Naaman.

When Naaman arrived at Elisha's, he sent a messenger to tell Naaman to wash in the river Jordan seven times. Naaman was angry, 'I thought Elisha would wave his hand over me and heal me. There are better rivers in Damascus, why can't I wash in them instead?' But Naaman's servants persuaded him to obey Elisha. He washed in the Jordan seven times and was healed. Naaman realised that Elisha's God was the true God and he decided to worship the true God from now on. We don't know what happened to the captive maid but it was thanks to her that Naaman came to believe in God.

 Top Tip: *God can use bad situations to make good things happen.*
'You have changed my sorrow into dancing. You took away my clothes of sadness and you have clothed me in garments of happiness.' Psalm 30:11

Joash (2 Kings 11; 2 Chronicles 22)

Joash's story is fascinating. He was very young when he became King of Judah and he became king in a very unusual way.

Joash's father was King Ahaziah who was encouraged to do wrong by the people who brought him up. Joash's grandmother was the wicked Athaliah. When Ahaziah died, Athaliah was determined to rule Judah instead and arranged to have the rest of the Royal family killed. However, one child escaped. The Princess Jehosheba, Ahaziah's sister, rescued Ahaziah's son, Joash.

The princess' husband, Jehoiada the priest, hid him in the temple for six years. During this time wicked Athaliah ruled the land. When Joash was seven years old Jehoiada said to all the priests, Levites and family leaders 'The king's son will rule. You priests and Levites go on duty on the Sabbath. A third of you will guard the doors, a third of you will be at the palace and a third at the foundation gate. All the other people will stay in the temple courtyards. No one can enter the temple except the priests and the Levites. The Levites must stay near the king to protect him, each man with a weapon in his hand.'

Joash was then crowned King of Israel. All the people shouted out 'Long live the king', and when Athaliah heard the noise she ran to see what had happened. When she saw the young king she tore her clothes and shouted out, 'Traitors! Traitors!' The soldiers of the new king surrounded Athaliah, dragged her out of the temple and killed her. Joash was very young to have so much responsibility but he had good advisers, unlike his father. He ruled the country for 40 years in Jerusalem and as long as the priest Jehoiada was alive, Joash did what was right and obeyed the Lord.

 Top Tip: *Thank God for good advice.*
'Your word is a lamp for my feet and a light for my path.' Psalm 119:105.

Hezekiah (2 Kings 18 and 19; 2 Chronicles 31:20-21)

Hezekiah was twenty five years old when he became king of Judah. His story is remarkable because he obeyed God and was successful. When Hezekiah had been on the throne for fourteen years Judah was attacked by Sennacherib, King of Assyria. Who was a proud and haughty man. When he surrounded Jerusalem he sent a message to the people, 'Don't listen to Hezekiah when he says "The Lord will save us."'

Hezekiah was very upset and sent an officer to the prophet Isaiah. Isaiah passed on God's message,

'Do not be frightened by the words of the king of Assyria... He will hear a report that will make him return to his own country and he will die by the sword there.' Then King Sennacherib sent another letter, 'Do not be fooled by the god you trust. Don't believe him when he says Jerusalem will not be handed over to the King of Assyria.'

Hezekiah asked God for help. He said 'The kings of Assyria have destroyed other countries. They have thrown their gods into the fire, but these gods were only statues that people made. Now, Lord our God, save us from this king's power so that all the kingdoms of the earth will know that you, Lord, are the only God.'

God then sent the angel of the Lord into the camp of the Assyrians - 185,000 Assyrian men died. When the remaining Assyrians got up next morning all they found were dead bodies. Sennacharib returned to his country where one day, as he worshipped in the temple of his god, he was killed with a sword by his own sons, just as God had said through the prophet Isaiah. Hezekiah was right to trust in the Lord.

Top Tip: *When people ridicule you for your faith in God remember how God protected Hezekiah. God's enemies never win... but Jesus also says...* 'Love your enemies and pray for those who hurt you.' Matthew 5:44.

Jabez (1 Chronicles 4:9-10)

We don't know much about Jabez. We know he was well respected and that his mother gave him the name Jabez because when she gave birth to him she was in a lot of pain. But Jabez is only mentioned in two verses in the Bible. So why is he mentioned at all? What did he do that is so amazing? Did he fight a battle or do something very clever? Did he make lots of money? Perhaps he did, but in God's plans winning wars, being clever or making money aren't really important. So what did Jabez do that pleased God? He prayed!

Jabez prayed to God, 'Please do good things for me and give me more land. Stay with me and don't let anyone hurt me. Then I won't have any pain.'

Perhaps the meaning of Jabez's name meant that Jabez was really worried about pain. He didn't want anyone to hurt or harm him. Jabez did the right thing with his worries, he brought them to God. He knew that when God was with him God would protect him. Jabez asked God to provide him with more land so that in the end he and his family would be well provided for.

It's not greedy to ask God for things - it's just rude if you only speak to God when you want something. God loves to give good things to his people but sometimes he says 'No' or 'Wait'. So what happened to Jabez? Did God answer his prayer? At the end of the verse we read, 'And God did what Jabez asked.' God can do that for you as well.

Top Tip: *Ask God for what you need and to forgive your sins.*
'For your name's sake, Lord, forgive my many sins.' Psalm 25:11

Jehoshaphat (2 Chronicles 19)

Jehoshaphat was King of Judah after his father Asa died and God was pleased with him as he followed his commands. One good thing Jehoshaphat did was to appoint judges in each of the fortified cities of Judah. Jehoshaphat told them to judge people carefully. 'Remember you are not judging for men but for the Lord. God is with you whenever you give a verdict. With God there is no injustice.'

Other legal disputes were to be dealt with by the priests, Levites or heads of families. Jehoshaphat told these men that whenever anyone came with a complaint or accusation or whenever anyone was accused of any crime they should warn those involved about the seriousness of sin. Disobeying God is wrong. It makes God angry. Jehoshaphat told the judges and officials to be brave. 'Act with courage,' he said 'and may the Lord be with those of you who do well.'

One army that came to fight Jehoshaphat was so huge that even he was frightened. Jehoshaphat told God that he didn't know what to do but that he would wait and see what God had in mind.

God said 'Do not be afraid or discouraged. The battle is not yours but mine. You will not even have to fight this battle. Watch how I will save you.'

As the army set out Jehoshaphat put his best singers out in front to sing praises to God. As they sang, God began to fight the enemy. When they arrived at the battle field all they saw was dead bodies. Everyone went home rejoicing. God had won again.

 Top Tip: *Remember that God is always the winner. He can even sort out our problems before we have to face them.*
'With God we will gain the victory.' Psalm 60:12

Mordecai (Esther 2 and 6)

Mordecai was a Jew who lived in the land of Persia when King Xerxes ruled the land. His story involves a king, an assassin and a beauty contest.

King Xerxes' wife Queen Vashti fell out with him and was banished from the palace leaving the position of queen vacant. A nationwide beauty contest was arranged so that the king could have his pick of all the beautiful young girls. Mordecai's orphan cousin, Esther, was extremely beautiful and when the announcement was made about the beauty contest Esther was taken to the palace along with many other girls.

The king chose Esther as his queen and Mordecai told her to keep her nationality secret. Jews were not liked by the Persians and if it was known that Esther was a Jew it might have changed the king's mind about her. So Esther didn't say anything and Mordecai walked past the king's courtyards every day to find out how she was. During one visit he overheard two men plotting to kill the king. Quickly he told Queen Esther who warned King Xerxes. But, Mordecai was forgotten... until one night when the king couldn't sleep.

He asked for the court record to be read to him and discovered that Mordecai had saved his life but had not been rewarded. The king honoured Mordecai by dressing him in royal robes and having him escorted on his own horse through the city. However Mordecai and the Jews were despised by the king's servant, Haman, who plotted to have them all killed. Thankfully God's plans meant that Esther was the queen. She was in the right place at the right time to save her people and her cousin Mordecai.

Top Tip: *Be where God wants you to be. Ask God to show you where you should be and be willing to work for him there.*
'The Lord's plans will stand for ever, his ideas will always last.' Psalm 33:11

Ebed Melech (Jeremiah 38)

Ebed Melech was not a Jew. He was a Cushite and a servant in King Zedekiah's palace in Judah. Ebed Melech was courageous and compassionate and saved the life of Jeremiah the prophet of the Lord God.

God was giving Jeremiah lots of things to say to the people of Judah. He told the people that Jerusalem would be destroyed and that they should all give themselves up to the invading Babylonian army. The army officials didn't like what they heard.

Jerusalem was being invaded because the people had forgotten God and had chosen to disobey him time and time again. Jeremiah just told everyone the truth, but people don't like to hear the truth when it makes them feel bad or guilty. The king's officers overheard Jeremiah's message and went to the king to complain. They told Zedekiah that something had to be done about Jeremiah. Zedekiah gave in and told them to do what they liked. 'Jeremiah is in your control. I cannot do anything to stop you,' he said. So the officers arrested Jeremiah and threw him into a deep muddy well to die.

Ebed Melech was angry about the bad way Jeremiah was treated. He ran to tell king Zedekiah what had happened.

Zedekiah was so ashamed to hear how Jeremiah had been treated that he allowed Ebed Melech to pull Jeremiah out of the well. Ebed Melech found some old rags which he threw down to Jeremiah. He told Jeremiah to place them under his arms to protect him from the rope and Jeremiah was then winched up to safety.

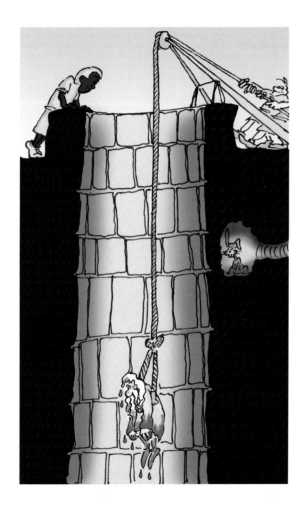

Top Tip: *Think about others. Ebed Melech was brave and thoughtful. You can help people in many different ways. The Bible says:* 'Do to other people what you want other people to do to you.' Matthew 7:12

Look out for the

other title in this series

Hall of Fame

New Testament

© 2000 Christian Focus Publications Ltd., Geanies House, Fearn,
Ross-shire, IV20 1TW, Scotland. www.christianfocus.com
Written by Catherine Mackenzie
Illustrated by Neil Stewart
All rights reserved, no part of this publication may be produced, stored in a retrieval
system, or transmitted, in any form or by any means, electronic, mechanical, photocopying
recording or otherwise without permission of Christian Focus Publications Ltd.